D0784273

Here for the first time in stark print are the poems of Attila the Stockbroker. After several hectic years of criss-crossing the country, bringing ranting verse and manic melodies to a growing and enthusiastic audience, Attila has taken time off to put together this first collection.

Russians; football; Albania; the spineless, wimpish anti-hero, Nigel; unemployment; the Miners' Strike and judges are just some of the themes that provoke Attila's funny, angry and popular verse.

Cautionary Tales
for
Dead Commuters

ATTILA THE STOCKBROKER
COLLECTED WORKS 1980—84 !!

with Illustrations
by Porky

London
UNWIN PAPERBACKS
Boston Sydney

Cautionary Tales for Dead Commuters first published
in this two book
collection in Great Britain by Unwin Paperbacks 1985

This book is copyright under the Berne Convention.
No reproduction
without permission. All rights reserved.

UNWIN® PAPERBACKS
40 Museum Street, London WC1A 1LU, UK
Unwin Paperbacks
Park Lane, Hemel Hempstead, Herts HP2 4TE, UK

George Allen & Unwin Australia Pty Ltd
8 Napier Street, North Sydney, NSW 2060, Australia

Unwin Paperbacks with the
Port Nicholson Press
PO Box 11–838 Wellington, New Zealand

© Attila the Stockbroker and Seething Wells, 1985
Illustrations © John Langford and Porky
Cover illustration: Porky

Designed by Graham Davis Associates
Designer Kevin Ryan
Assistant Sara Woollcombe
Typeset by Dawkins Typesetters, London

Poems

HeLLO!

And so, after several years charging round the country taking ranting verse and manic mandola melodies to the parts most Serious Literature doesn't reach, I've splattered the words on the page for all the world to see. I'm not interested in Poetry as Art if it means obscure cerebral celebrations by seven people in some grant assisted wine glass-strewn ghetto; I want to write words which make people laugh out loud in packed train compartments, words which are passed round the crowd at half time at football matches, performed in pubs and colleges, printed in fanzines, enjoyed in schools. I write and perform for my audiences, not a few critics sitting in armchairs in their safe European homes. SOD THE MUSE, LET'S MAKE THE NEWS!

This collection is dedicated above all to the memory of my father Bill, himself a poet (though not a ranter!). His heart was in words; he taught me to appreciate them, and though he died when I was ten his spirit lives on in every word that I write. Also to my mother for her unstinting if slightly uncomprehending support over the years – I did try to wear a suit, Mum, but it just wouldn't fit . . . Without Porky Jupitus's cartoons these poems would only be half alive and if there's any justice in the world this guy has a massive dose of success awaiting him. And thanks to Joy Scully and Mary Clarke for all the friendship, encouragement and typing and to Lynne and Redruth Lomond for their human and musical support and for driving me all over the place in cars of varying roadworthiness . . . Hi to Steve Drewett and the Newtown Neurotics, everyone at Brighton & Hove Albion F.C., all my friends in Harlow and Brighton and all the rest from Tyne & Wear to Cornwall and overseas, Garry Bushell, Andy from Ruislip, all the Ranters, Billy Bragg, Brian Patten and Roger McGough, John and Linda, Cor in Holland, everyone in Albania especially the glorious ghost of Uncle Enver (and Alexei Sayle who shares my silly love of the Glorious People's Republic – we were once in the same Albania – admiring left wing party) Monty Python, the ghosts of Lenny Bruce and Hilaire Belloc and flatfish everywhere . . . Last but not least to my companion at arms Seething Wells – here's hoping it sells millions!

If you enjoy this book, you might also like a copy of TIRANA THRASH, the legendary Albanian ranting poetry fanzine featuring new writers and poets from all over Britain (and, yes, a few from Albania as well). It's available from me for 50p + large SAE c/o George Allen & Unwin, 40 Museum Street, London WC1A 1LU. If you have any comments about the book please write – your views are extremely important to me and if you send an SAE you'll definitely get a reply. To finish; I hope you enjoy reading these words as much as I've enjoyed writing and performing them over the last few years. And Porky says the same too, from the bottom of his gut . . .

Attila, Spring 1985

****

ROOTS, ROCK, WOMBLES.

Attila the Stockbroker also has two LPs available; the first, 'Ranting At The Nation' (released March '83), contains live recordings of much of the material in this book including 'Awayday' and the Russians series, as well as some songs and silly sketches recorded in the studio. The second, 'Sawdust and Empire' (released May '84) is an LP of mostly serious songs: the lyrics of the title track and 'Factory Gods' are reproduced herein. If you are interested in either of these opuses contact CHERRY RED RECORDS/ANAGRAM RECORDS, 49–53 Kensington Gardens Square, London W2.
All song lyrics are published by kind permission of Cherry Red Music Ltd.

GlosSarY

(for those who don't share my strangely twisted view of the world!)

ALBANIA – a very silly country on the Adriatic coast. Population around three million, mostly tractors. Main industry – halibut farming.

BROMLEY – a graveyard in Kent. Dead people live there.

CRASS – a very noisy, very angry anarchist punk band, prime exponents of the repeated and virtually exclusive use of expletives as a form of human communication.

COMMUTERS – dead people in suits. Live in Bromley (cf).

DHSS – the dole office (for foreign readers).
The one growth industry in
Britain today.

DYNAMO KIEV – the pride of Soviet football. Feared from Moscow to Minsk.

ENVER HOXHA – pronounced HODGER – the beloved leader of the Albanian people, beloved son of the Albanian soil, source of all wisdom, enemy of Yugoslav revisionism and defender of the halibut farms. Shoots people at his Cabinet meetings. Recently departed to the great tractor factory in the sky, but still the most ideologically sound man in the solar system.

TRISTAN AND ENVER

EXISTENTIALISM – a philosophy of life.
Independence and Lager!

HENLEY REGATTA – annual rich bigots' binge, reputedly funded by Colonel Gaddafy (now THAT should get them annoyed!).

MILLWALL – very nasty South London football team . . . even harder than Seething Wells!

NIGEL – a stateless and spineless wimp who found immortality!

JOHN PEEL – the opposite of Steve Wright, a veritable hero and star radio DJ (with a lousy taste in football teams).

RADIO ONE – the most boring radio station in the galaxy. Makes Radio Moscow sound like Monty Python . . .

THE SUN – a target beloved of Ranters everywhere, and with good reason. Anyone who reads this newspaper is even more of a prat than your average Crystal Palace fan. And that's saying something!

TRISTAN – pet flounder of Enver Hoxha (see above). The most politically advanced flatfish in contemporary history.

WOMBLES – nasty little creatures with axes, reputed to live on Wimbledon Common.

STEVE WRIGHT – a wombat, somehow transplanted from the Australian outback into the corridors of Radio One (cf).

"AND IM ALRIGHT"

EVERY TIME I EAT VEGETABLES . . .

No agony, no ecstasy, no pleasure and no pain –
so exquisitely uninteresting you drive your wife insane
The TV is your oracle, the newspapers your guide
and your shiny little vehicle is your passion and your pride
You've done the same things every day for nigh on forty years
and in your ludicrous routines you hide your worthless fears
On the blandest boat in Boredom you are captain of the crew –
and every time I eat vegetables it makes me think of you.

You died the day that you were born and now you sit and rot
a three-piece-suited dinosaur in the pond that time forgot . . .
Your image is respectable, there's nothing underneath
and the whole thing is as surely false as Esther Rantzen's teeth
Your views are carbon copies of the rubbish that you read
and you swallow every morsel Rupert Murdoch seeks to feed
You go to bed at ten because you've nothing else to do
and every time I eat vegetables it makes me think of you.

And now a few choice words without the slightest hint of malice –
rather than spend the day with you I'd play for Crystal Palace!
I really love your company when you are far away
and I'll go there tomorrow if you're going there today
If you love the establishment as much as you declare
then go to a cruise missile base and establish yourself there . . .
You're the middle-aged equivalent of a kid who's sniffing glue
and every time I eat vegetables it makes me think of you.

You're a cabbage in a pickle and your brain has sprung a leek
so lettuce keep our distance 'cos I vomit when you speak
I'll always do a runner so I'm going where you've bean
'cos to see you chills my marrow and turns my tomatoes green
You're an eighteen carrot cretin with a dandelion whine –
so stick to your herbaceous border and I'll stick to mine
and although this verse is corny, it's amaizing but it's true
that every time I eat vegetables it makes me think of you!

THEY MUST BE... Яussians!

They slither round corners with scarves round their faces
they always turn up in improbable places
they lack the good taste of the British, our graces
they're horrid — they must be the Яussians!

They're always involved in some dastardly plot
they're never content with whatever they've got
and they are the cause of the Great British Rot!
they're horrid — they must be the Яussians!

They sit in the Hilton and scowl at the waiters
they drink a foul potion distilled from potatoes
and everyone knows they detest us and hate us
they're horrid — they must be the Яussians!

They've Benn and the Trots who all want to enslave us
and countless Red spies who all want to deprave us
but Maggie's alright — she'll defend us and save us
from the muggers from Moscow, the Яussians!

And her mate in the White House, a fine manly figure
he knows how to handle a Jew or a nigger
when Maggie gets Trident and Яon gets the trigger
we'll give 'em DETEЯЯENT, those Яussians!

Oh, hang on a minute — my brain's on the blink
I think that the Kremlin's been spiking my drink
How unpatriotic! I've started to THINK!
It must be all down to the Яussians . . .

My mate here just told me they've got a new plan
they're holding a party in Afghanistan
and he's got an invite, as number one fan
they can't all be horrid, the Яussians!

12

Hey, look – over there – they're down in the park
they're holding a meeting out there in the dark
the speaker looks just like that *John Cooper Clarke* –
they all dress so formal, the Яussians . . .

I'm going to meet them; I want to be friends
find out if they follow the West's latest trends
and have long discussions, the means and the ends –
I'm getting quite fond of the Яussians . . .

Hey, hang on – they're smiling and there's music playing!
– Sounds like *the Redskins* – oh, I feel like staying!
They're handing out ice cream, and bopping, and swaying –
I THINK I'LL GO BACK WITH THE ЯUSSIANS!

And if there's one thing that the Great British Press hate more than the RUSSIANS, it's got to be the SOCIAL SECURITY SCROUNGERS . . .

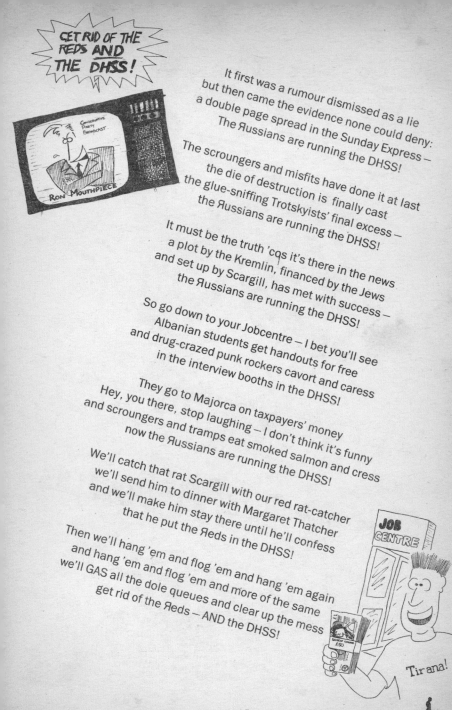

GET RID OF THE REDS AND THE DHSS!

RON MOUTHPIECE

It first was a rumour dismissed as a lie
but then came the evidence none could deny:
a double page spread in the Sunday Express –
The Яussians are running the DHSS!

The scroungers and misfits have done it at last
the die of destruction is finally cast
the glue-sniffing Trotskyists' final excess –
the Яussians are running the DHSS!

It must be the truth 'cqs it's there in the news
a plot by the Kremlin, financed by the Jews
and set up by Scargill, has met with success –
the Яussians are running the DHSS!

So go down to your Jobcentre – I bet you'll see
Albanian students get handouts for free
and drug-crazed punk rockers cavort and caress
in the interview booths in the DHSS!

They go to Majorca on taxpayers' money
Hey, you there, stop laughing – I don't think it's funny
and scroungers and tramps eat smoked salmon and cress
now the Яussians are running the DHSS!

We'll catch that rat Scargill with our red rat-catcher
we'll send him to dinner with Margaret Thatcher
and we'll make him stay there until he'll confess
that he put the Яeds in the DHSS!

Then we'll hang 'em and flog 'em and hang 'em again
and hang 'em and flog 'em and more of the same
we'll GAS all the dole queues and clear up the mess
get rid of the Яeds – AND the DHSS!

JOB CENTRE

Tirana!

15

And the RUSSIANS aren't finished yet – they've taken over the greatest bastion of American civilisation – – –

ЯUSSIANS IN McDONALDS

Startled shoppers stand and stare
in the burger joint in Leicester Square
a cold Siberian close encounter
Muscovites behind the counter
and Georgian ladies with massive hips
serve Brezhnevburger and double chips
This is the Kremlin's latest ploy –
a difference at Mcdonalds you'll ЯEALLY enjoy!

16

The hammer and sickle above the door
says 'Yanks not welcome any more'
no more piped musak oh so dire
now they've a full Яed Army choir
The KGB are eating in

they're kicking up a fearful din
the door guard bellows 'SHUT THAT NOISE!'
the commissar says 'Purge him, boys!'

The stars and stripes hang upside down
the Queen is green and wears a frown
but Lenin hangs there high and proud
staring at the burger crowd . . .
The American Secretary of Defense
(a man who causes great offence)
is minced and served with garlic cheese
'cos Casper Weinburgers really please!

The Pentagon's in disarray
the news has filtered through today
and Alex Haig looks really vexed —
'The Яeds'll have the Wimpys next!'
And here's more news that's really hot:
J. Я. Ewing is a Trot!
Neil Diamond's played Angola —
and Marx invented Coca Cola . . .

Western values fade and die
as Яed successes multiply
Arthur Miller isn't dead
he's writing radio plays instead
and as the bastions crash and fall
here comes the greatest blow of all:
it took a long time to deduce
but Яeagan's really . . . Lenny Bruce!

ON THE BENCHES, IN THE COURTROOMS, ITS THE
GERIATRICS RATHER THAN THE LUNATICS WHO
HAVE TAKEN OVER THE ASYLUM. . . .

 A

DAY

IN

THE

 LIFE

The flecks of spit are wiped away —
I fade into another day
the rolling eyes and trembling hands
eroded by time's ruthless sands
the tongue lolls wide, the voice is weak
a whisper fading to a squeak
the nurse bends over, hands so cool
and wipes away the dribble pool

I know full well my time is nigh
and hope I'm not afraid to die —
or so I feel when mind is clear
for mostly I'm not really here
but life for me was good and long
I did my best, knew right from wrong
and served my land with heart and brain
I'd love to have my time again . . .

A gentle hand; a muffled curse
'Oh, can't you see I'm resting, Nurse?'
'Now come on love, your breakfast tray
and sit up straight — it's your big day
I'll wipe your nose if you keep still
so drink your drink and take your pill
and when I've washed you, combed your hair
we'll get you dressed and find your chair . . .'

Now it's the wheelchair — and the lift
with Fred the porter, morning shift
I want to go back to the ward
but all my protests are ignored
the ambulance doors open wide —
it's up the ramp and soon inside
the nurse smiles sweetly, holds my hand
I whisper 'I don't understand'!

The Minister unlocks his case —
speaks carefully into my face
'The money's in your Swiss account
your great grandson checked the amount
and here's the tape of what to say —
you've got a big one up today
Appeal Court case; GCHQ
now we must go; your verdict's due . . .'

For Judge Richards, who said that a woman who was raped while hitchhiking in Ipswich late at night was 'asking for it' and guilty of contributory negligence. The man who raped her got off with a fine

CONTRIBUTORY

Hitching up the M I I
coming back from a Dexys gig
got picked up 'bout half eleven
by this bloke in a funny wig
flash Mercedes, new and gleaming
deep pile seats and deep seat piles
I got in and sat there scheming
while the fat cat flashed me smiles

Told me he was back from Sessions
with a load of ageing hacks
told me he'd made no concessions
to the bootboys and the blacks
said he thought that it was stupid
fuss 'bout rapists on the news
bloke was only playing Cupid
girls like that they don't refuse

Asked me if I thought him enemy
asked me if I bore a grudge
told me that he came from Henley
said he was a High Court judge
I asked him to stop a second
'Need a slash' that's what I said
when he did the anger beckoned
and I smacked him in the head

NEGLIGENCE

took the keys and took his money
smashed the car into a ditch
though he moaned 'They'll get you, sonny'
got away without a hitch
I don't think they'll ever find me
'cos I'm many miles away
but if one day they're right behind me
I know what I'm gonna say –

HE ASKED FOR IT! He's rich and snobbish
right wing, racist, sexist too!
Fat and ugly, sick and slobbish –
should be locked in London Zoo!
He wanted me to beat him up!
It was an open invitation!
Late at night he picked me up –
an act of open provocation!

High Court judges are a blight
They should stay at home in nice warm beds
and if they must drive late at night
should never pick up Harlow Reds!
A five pence fine is right and proper –
and to sum up my defence
it was his fault he came a cropper:
CONTRIBUTORY NEGLIGENCE!

In early 1982 an infamous decision by five Law
Lords declared the Greater London Council's
cheap fares policy illegal — despite the fact
that millions of Londoners had voted for it. Many
people considered this decision to be, er, a bit
undemocratic . . .

AWAYDAY

Woke up got up read the post attacked the postman took the rat for a walk
came back fed the amoeba made some coffee wrote a passionate love letter
to shirley williams enclosing a small dead animal then thought i'm bored
think i'll go to london 'cos london's more interesting than harlow and i
might be able to pick up some bucks fizz bootlegs or the latest jean-paul
sartre dub lp got the bus ten minutes late got the train twenty minutes late
train was delayed for two hours due to dead liberals on the line got to london
liverpool street went down the tube stepping on unsuspecting commuters
all the way up to the ticket booth single to covent garden please sure mate
that'll be five pound fifty what do you mean five pound fifty it was only
twenty pence yesterday i'm not paying five pound fifty to go to covent
garden from liverpool street sorry mate i know it was only twenty pence
yesterday but a ninety-seven-year-old deaf geriatric ostrich-minded
extremely rich archaic obsolete semi-senile reactionary friedman-
worshipping member of an outdated unnecessary and entirely superfluous
elitist and oligarchic institution who never uses the tube anyway 'cos he's
got a fucking chauffeur-driven limousine woke up with a headache in the
middle of last night and decided to increase london fares by two thousand
per cent and got four of his senile friends to agree with him – posthumously
– and so we've had to put the fares up that's called freedom democracy the
rule of law and defending the british way of life that'll be five pound fifty
please . . .

BOLLOCKS TO THAT i said and after a short pregnant pause all the people behind me in the queue plucked up courage and said BOLLOCKS TO THAT and all the pinstripe-and-soda brigade coming down the stairs said BOLLOCKS TO THAT and all the other people at liverpool street underground and at the bus stops said BOLLOCKS TO THAT apart from the nice polite human league and smiths fans who thought it was rude to say BOLLOCKS but when it was revealed to them that in the famous sex pistols lp cover trial of 1977 a high court judge had ruled that BOLLOCKS was not an obscene word then they too said BOLLOCKS TO THAT and soon the entire length and breadth of the london transport network was full of people saying BOLLOCKS TO THAT and refusing to pay the increased fares and when finally a large crowd of completely sober and totally moderate forty-nine-year-old lloyds underwriters called brian started going up to yer average law lord in the street saying BOLLOCKS TO THAT and hitting him over the head with a large mallet the powers that be decided to abandon the fares increase in the interests of public safety and then everything went back to normal but it made me wonder so i'm forming a mass revolutionary party and our slogan manifesto and programme is going to be BOLLOCKS TO THAT!

nigel wants to go to C&A's
but it's been taken over by the viet cong
and nigel doesn't like the viet cong

****

nigel wants to go to C&A's
but a chapter of hell's angels are playing scrabble
    with the viet cong
and nigel doesn't like hell's angels

****

nigel wants to go to C&A's
but the toilets are full of Crass fans
and nigel doesn't like Crass fans

****

nigel wants to go to C&A's
but the women's institute have organised an orgy in
    the bedding department
and nigel doesn't like orgies

****

nigel wants to go to C&A's
but the lifts are full of albanian footballers
and nigel doesn't like albanian footballers

****

nigel wants to go to C&A's
but the menswear department is full of existentialists
and nigel doesn't like existentialists
not even part-time ones

****

nigel wants to go to C&A's
but I don't understand why
'cos they don't sell nerve gas in C&A's
not even to SDP members in cashmere sweaters . . .

I DON'T TALK TO POP STARS

I don't talk to pop stars
and they don't talk to me
it's a mutual arrangement —
the way we like to be
I don't talk to pop stars
they make me feel depressed
and I won't sit in dressing rooms
and watch them get undressed
I don't talk to pop stars
they really piss me off
I hope they die in poverty
like poor Vincent van Gogh
I don't talk to pop stars
and I hope that you don't too
'cos if you've talked to Billy Bragg
then I won't talk to you
I don't talk to pop stars
won't share their cans of beer
I never nick their underpants
I'd better make that clear
I don't talk to pop stars
I think they should be shot
or gassed, or hung, or sterilised
or the whole bloody lot
I don't talk to pop stars
they really make me sick
especially that Seething Wells
he really is a prick
I don't talk to pop stars
they really make me vomit
I'd rather clean out lavatories
or study Halley's comet
I don't talk to pop stars
I wish they'd go away
and I walk out of pop concerts
when pop stars start to play
I don't talk to pop stars
but listen to my plea —
one day, when I'm a pop star,
will you still talk to me?

30

Michael Fagan, a friendly but eccentric soul, pays a personal visit to the Queen in her own bedroom at Buckingham Palace and steals half a bottle of wine. All hell breaks loose...

THE PERILS OF STEALING HALF A BOTTLE OF WINE

Three o'clock in the afternoon feeling really pissed off the jean-paul sartre dub lp featuring jah schopenhauer is awful and the bucks fizz bootlegs aren't bucks fizz at all they're crass live at the tory party conference and to crown it all there isn't even any albanian football on the telly right i think i'll go and get drunk i've never done that before pubs aren't open so it's down to the off licence past c&a's hello nigel no nigel put that nail bomb away i'm not the prat who writes nasty things about you into the off licence ten crates of fosters and half a bottle of wine for my pet halibut maxwell on the way to the checkout desk realise i haven't got enough money so i slip the wine under my jacket and smile sweetly at the till operator all goes well until i trip over the serious poetry reading being held by the door and crash forward revealing the offending bottle you thieving scum shouts the shop manager i'll have your scrotal sac for this as he holds me in a vicelike grip and dials the police with his free hand ten meat wagons three armoured cars a detachment of the sas and five harrier jump jets storm the building and as i'm seized and taken into custody i'm astonished at the commotion until suddenly i realise that i'm going to be charged with stealing half a bottle of wine and the going rate for stealing half a bottle of wine is three years of intensive electric shock treatment and ice baths in solitary confinement followed by twenty years in the mental hospital of your choice with the option of being experimented on in a vivisection clinic and playing endless games of chess with sterilised monkeys so i think to myself as i'm led away that next time i won't steal half a bottle of wine i'll try something less dangerous like rape tax embezzlement fraud or property speculation 'cos no one worries about things like that do they. . . .

nigel wants to go and see simple minds
they're playing at the camden palace
and nigel likes the camden palace

****

nigel wants to go and see simple minds
they're supporting the smiths
and nigel likes the smiths
(though not as much as simple minds)

****

nigel wants to go and see simple minds
the singer's got a funny voice
and nigel likes funny voices

****

nigel wants to go and see simple minds
the singer's got a funny haircut
and nigel likes funny haircuts

★★★★★★★★★★★★★★★★★★★★★★★★★

nigel wants to go and see simple minds
they play nice, bland, unchallenging pop music
and nigel likes nice, bland, unchallenging pop music
(that's why he likes simple minds)

★★★★★★★★★★★★★★★★★★★★★★★★★

nigel wants to go and see simple minds
but he's just found out that he can't go
because of the SDP grave robbing party
(still, there's always next year)

Dating from my days in the Stock Exchange, this is a rant about boring, grey people who gather in City wine bars after office hours and whinge about things they don't understand.

GENTLEMEN
OF THE

WRIST

In a shitty city wine bar whining in their wine about rates and dates and druggers and muggers and red ken and his men and dirty diners and militant miners they slob out the evening in sweaty pinheaded pinstriped pissed up pathetic postures paranoid penpushers on parole gin-and-tonic really chronic quite moronic want to be bionic but whoever heard of a bionic bank clerk wouldn't that be a lark the nightly convention of the highly conventional order of the gentlemen of the wrist brackets pissed spews the news and blows a fuse they whinge and binge and singe their minge eric should have been home two hours ago his wife will kill him but it's his round so he's staying around the eighth pint's been downed and the first one to be sick is a prick so give it some stick mick 'cos eric's a real MAN and he can hold his lukewarm watneys better than you can heard the one about the queer irish jew locked in the loo ha ha great mate give us another before we go home to one mother or another look over there that bird is the word could really poke that no don't be an absurd nurd don't be a twat that's too fat time to go see you tomorrow have a good pube on the tube but watch out for the niggers and the liggers and the nightly convention of the highly conventional order of the gentlemen of the wrist brackets pissed is dismissed home to the wife who says hallo little wife where have you been you smell obscene it's plainly seen you're no james dean what's that you said who's in our bed that's your brother he's my lover four hours late food's on the plate I didn't wait HERO ZERO eight hours work five hours drinking five seconds thinking time for sleep for suburban sheep off to bed empty head might as well be DEAD!

ALBANIAN FOOTBALL

<u>This one's about a subject very dear to my heart</u>

Oh sun-kissed waves, carry me across the bay
to the place where the glorious Partizani Tirana play
The lure of the fresh-mined beaches; the roar of the crowd
the clatter of the machine-guns when someone shouts too loud . . .
My memory goes back to classic games
and tears well at those old familiar names:
Nendori Tirana, Dinamo Tirana too
in the Qemal Stafa Stadium where the red flags always flew . . .
Traktori Korça sadly got locked up
for losing to revisionists in the European Cup
and as for poor old Durres, the team that time forgot
they finished bottom of the league – and so they all got shot!
But a source of inspiration and the country's greatest pride
are the marvellous achievements of the People's National Side
Their manager's the President, his name is Enver Hoxha
he's a bit of a dictator but he's not a bad old codger
and there's nothing to put spice into the fight against relegation
like knowing that the penalty is instant liquidation . . .
There are many countries in a state of constant football mania
but you'll find they've really got the killer instinct in Albania!

HOLIDAY
in Albania

(AN ALBANIAN 12 BAR BLUES)

I don't want a fortnight on the Costa del Sol
Don't wanna go to Bognor – it's a plague-ridden hole
and it don't fit in with my ideology . . .
Down the Adriatic to the Vlora bay
Twenty pints of Fosters and I'm away
'Cos now I know just where I wanna be:
Albania – that's the place for me!

Used to like Bermuda but there's too many lice
and last year I caught herpes and that's not very nice
so take me where the lemmings all run free . . .
We'll boogie in Tirana to the latest sounds
Then to Gjirokastra and we'll do the rounds
'Cos now I know just where I wanna be:
Albania – that's the place for me!

There really isn't anything to match the charms
of the tractor factories and the halibut farms
and the legendary football team, Partizani!
I don't want a holiday in the sun –
two weeks in Albania's much more fun
and now I know just where I wanna be:
Albania – that's the place for me!
Said ALBANIA – that's the place for me!

For all those who listen
to short wave radio — and
especially to Radio Tirana,
glorious mouthpiece of
the Albanian people
(it really does sound
like this, by the way)

A VERY SILLY EAST EUROPEAN PROPAGANDA STATION

Long live the People's Socialist Republic of Albania
under the correct leadership of the
Party of Labour of Albania with Comrade Enver Hoxha
at the head!
Long live the steel-like unity of the Albanian workers,
peasants and people's intellectuals
around their beloved party as they carry forward
the bright red banner of socialism
and win ever more brilliant victories in the construction
of the socialist homeland!
Victory to Marxism-Leninism, an ever-correct
and scientific doctrine and an iron-forged weapon
in the hands of the progressive peoples!
Death to American imperialism, Soviet social-imperialism
Chinese revisionism, colonialism,
neo-colonialism and the traitorous activities
of the Yugoslav revisionist plotters,
their lackeys, running dogs and HALIBUTS!
Long live Comrade Enver Hoxha, beloved son
of the Albanian soil,
and his pet flounder, TRISTAN!
Victory to people's war and the liberation movements of the world
under the correct leadership of
RODDY THE RAGWORM!
Long live the people's electrification, socialist collectivisation
and LARRY THE LUGWORM!
The wombats have nothing to lose but their bondage trousers!
Wombats of all countries, unite!
And to end our very silly broadcast, here is a poem:
Stalin had a little lamb —
it gave him naughty urges
so he tied it to a five-bar gate
and shot it in the purges . . . .

SUN READERS

This lot had the sheer temerity to come to Wembley and beat England on our own patch in a match we had to win to be sure of qualifying for the European Championship finals . . . .

VOMIT ON A VIKING

The danes the danes we'll bash their brains and wire their willies to the mains boycott their bacon and their prawns and go and piss over their lawns the scabby scandinavian scum got scrotal scabies in the bum they live on fish heads and weak tea their lager tastes like canine pee you put a spanner in the works you slimy sweaty foreign berks you beat our lads we'll have your nuts we rule the waves no ifs and buts I know that we played worse than crewe and half the team were high on glue but you'd no right to spoil our day no foreign puffs get in our way your greasy fans with greasy smells swarmed through our streets and our hotels and then the alcoholic grubs drank all the carlsberg in the pubs we know just how you won you scabs you bribed the ref with porno mags and so our forwards wouldn't shoot you gave them whips and bondage suits but shut your mouths and stop your jibes and stuff your filthy porno bribes you may have had your greatest wish but sod off home and eat your fish!

Some time later the revolting and slimy Danes went into their last match in Athens, needing to win to qualify for the finals. They did, thanks to a truly pathetic performance by the home team. And so . . .

TAKE A LEAK ON A GREEK

The greeks the greeks we'll slap their cheeks and lock them up in bogs for weeks puke in their restaurants and bars and write rude slogans on their cars the spineless apathetic prats played like a bunch of dead wombats with all the vigour of a bit of week-old anaconda shit we needed you to win you slobs to beat the danes and shut their gobs knock out the greasy fishy turds and make

FOOTBALL PAGE

them eat their slimy words you useless cretins went and
lost and now you're gonna count the cost we're out of
europe thanks to you I'll tell you what we're gonna do
we'll get a load of herpes scabs and stick 'em all in
your kebabs put demis roussos on a diet go to corfu and
start a riot and here's the real ace up our sleeve
something you surely won't believe over your borders
will rampage albanian armies in a rage you slimy wimps
just lost your nerve your manager's a filthy perv you
let us down you didn't try it isn't fair I'M GONNA
CRY. . .

But now, of course, things are on the upturn with a vengeance; the third rant in the
trilogy celebrates a famous victory and gives new meaning to the expression 'a right
Turkey...'

SPEW UPON A SARACEN

The turks the turks you useless jerks you sit and weep
while england smirks the worst display I've ever seen
from any kind of football team I've got one thing to say
to you you're worse then cyprus and corfu and
luxembourg and lichtenstein your uselessness I can't
define your players should be smeared with jam and made
to mime on stage with wham! or forced to swallow
paraquat and climb right up mount ararat a half dead
sloth in bondage gear with creeping herpes of the ear
would have put up a good display compared to what you did
that day and as for england what a team now we can all
share robson's dream as here before our very eyes our
world cup willies start to rise oh shit I mean our hopes
of course but anyway we're out in force and on our way to
mexico to flagellate the foreign foe its turkey 0 and
england 8 so let's go out and celebrate get drunk fall
down and do the works and throw up over passing turks and
just one thing before I go a thing all turkish fans
should know predictable meant to embarrass YOU'RE EVEN
WORSE THAN CRYSTAL PALACE!

THE Scum

ANOTHER SCUM EXCLUSIVE

THE NIGHT I SLEPT WITH SEETHING WELLS

A far-off town and a late night bash
and a double bed was our place to crash
so listen here 'cos this story tells
of the night I slept with Seething Wells · · ·

I didn't mind — or so I said
but I wish I'd had the floor instead
'cos you'd never imagine the thousand hells
of a night in bed with Seething Wells · · ·

When he got undressed I had to retreat
from his shaven head and his mouldy feet —
the feet that launched a thousand smells
in that fragrant night with Seething Wells!

So I kept right close to the edge of the bed
and I pulled the blankets over my head
but eerie snores and stifled yells
soon woke me, thanks to Seething Wells

and, turning, I came face to face
with a massive boil in a private place
and a couple of hairy bagatelles
made me run like hell from Seething Wells · · ·

and I vowed right then that if need be
I'd spend the night in a cemetery
or sleep with dogs, or DEAD GAZELLES —
but never again with Seething Wells!

This rant is about dead commuters – or, more accurately, about the very small difference between dead commuters and live ones.

Deep in the dingy dirty decomposing dog shit-dripping dungeon of a graffiti-graced southern region train compartment stuffed full of bad-breath-breathing halibut-eyed computer commuters with boring suits and boring habits the state of play is giving cause for concern the middle-aged middle-class middle-management middle-everything puke-suited slack-jawed suet-pudding-faced powell-worshipping willie whitelaw clone by the window is slumped rigidly over his daily telegraph in a posture indicating his sudden demise this alarms the prim po-faced clean-tablecloth-every-night sex-in-the-dark-once-a-week daily-mail-female secretary by his side who asks him politely if he recently died receiving no reply she turns to the lard-assed times-reading tory-voting pinstriped wimp sitting opposite and demands an opinion in company with the three paul eddington clones also occupying the compartment he lowers his eyes and stares fixedly at his newspaper in the time honoured fashion of the don't-pinch-my-seat-don't-invade-my-world-I'm-all-right-jack-leave-me-alone-english suburban commuter husbands club she turns to me and confidently I tell her that most commuters are dead it's their natural state and anyway dead executives can't possibly be any less interesting than live ones though I can see that they might smell a bit more and that's why they always get aftershave for christmas and anyway I'm never going to bromley again unless I become an undertaker or join the SDP which is roughly the same thing . . . .

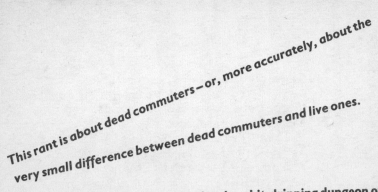

Nigel wants to

Nigel went to C&A's
walked around in a doped-up haze
Nigel went to see Simple Minds
always ate his bacon rinds
till one day feeling quite insane
he took a trip down Cold Blow Lane
and now—believe this if you can—
he's turned into a Millwall fan!

Those Crass fans they don't scare him now
he's always getting in a row
and existentialists run away
'My god—it's Nige!' you'll hear them say
He's got the latest Damned LP
and he's right off the Funboy Three:
a final proof of his disorder—
he's sold his bootlegs of New Order!

No more long macs with tatty hems
he's got a new pair of DMs
and since his notoriety's spreading
he's gone headbanging down at Reading!
And now—a thing you'll never guess—
he wants to join the SAS
and wear a silly rubber suit
and teach the Argies how to shoot ...

Yes, Nigel's hard—as hard as nails
and I could tell some awesome tales
like how he turned up all alone
took West Ham North Bank on his own
True, it was three o'clock at night
and there was no one there to fight
but listen hard to my advice—
Don't mess with Nigel: HE'S NOT NICE!

Many people have said that ranting verse isn't Real Poetry at all. Just to prove that I can write Great Literature with the best of them, here's a poem in the great British Poetry tradition – dedicated to British Bards throughout the ages, like the one in the cartoon . . .

My Wardrobe

My wardrobe is like a garden
but there's jackets instead of the snails
and instead of the trees there's jeans with no knees
and instead of the birdshit there's rails

My wardrobe is like a garden
but there's hangers instead of the grass
and instead of the fence there's a stray twenty pence
in a suit with a hole in the arse

My wardrobe is like a garden
but there's Y fronts instead of the dirt
and instead of the stems there's a pair of DMs
and instead of the leaves there's a shirt

My wardrobe is like a garden
but instead of the flowers there's socks
and instead of the heather there's vests made of leather
and a whip that I keep in a box

My wardrobe is like a garden
oh, I don't know how I've got the gall
my wardrobe is just like a wardrobe –
it's not like a garden at all!

FLEET STREET
FIGHTING MAN

This is about the

prostitutes of Fleet Street;

the gin-soaked, semi-

literate, shit-mongering

'journalists' who have

sold themselves

body and soul and

slavishly regurgitate

the same reactionary gutter

crap week in, week out . . .

GROTESQUE AT A DESK BURLESQUE YELLOW AS VOMIT
COWARDLY AS THE TWENTY-TO-ONE LONG SHOT
THIN BLUE GANG THAT'S FLEET STREET FIGHTING MAN
SCUMMY WHORE HIRELING OF THE MEDIA ELITE
SYCOPHANTIC MINDFUCKED TOAD-KISSING SLUG PROPRIETOR'S FEET
YOU CAME OUT OF COLLEGE SURE YOU'D BE A STAR
BUT LOOK AT YOUR MASTERS AND SEE WHO THEY ARE
MURDOCH AND MAXWELL AND THATCHER AND ALL
AND YOU SIT THERE WHINGEING AT THEIR BECK AND CALL
CLICHE PAP CRAP CHURNED OUT FOR THE NATION
REACTIONARY GARBAGE AND WORD MASTURBATION
YOUTH CULTURE STEREOTYPE SKINHEAD PUNK VANDAL
RACE CULTURE STEREOTYPE BLACK MUGGER SCANDAL
HOW MANY LIVES HAVE YOU RUINED WITH YOUR LIES
KING OF THE SEWER LORD OF THE FLIES
YOU CONTEMPTIBLE QUISLING YOU CHEAP PLASTIC GOEBBELS
YOU ARSELICKING UNCLE SAM EDITOR'S TOADY
YOU'VE NO PERSONALITY YOU'RE JUST A SLOB
WHO'D WRITE ANYTHING TO KEEP YOUR STINKING JOB
YOUR BRAIN STINKS OF MARSH GAS YOUR PEN STINKS OF SHIT
LOOK ROUND FOR THE CESSPOOL YOU'RE STANDING IN IT!

FURNITURE

Your mode is in the passive, you're a person by default
when you were born your parents took you with a pinch of salt
and now you sit there moaning at the image on your screen
an extension of your armchair is all that you've ever been
The kindest thing to say about you is that you're still alive
Your workmates will confirm this fact, at least from nine to five
and as you bleat at Scargill so distaste and shock combine –
'cos I thought you were the furniture until I heard you whine . . .

Your sex life is a catalogue of your poor wife's frustrations –
like thousands of Red Indians, she has her reservations
so you sit there and play the bigot just like all the others
who fake authoritarian postures 'cos they're lousy lovers
and if you had some SPIRIT then it wouldn't be so bad;
it's your awesome anonymity which makes me get so mad
Your brain stem is a nether world where boring cells combine
and I thought you were the furniture until I heard you whine

The great silent majority, that's you – I know it well
but I don't play the numbers game; you can still go to hell
you obviously don't want to LIVE, so shrivel up and die
and read your Sun or Telegraph in the snug bar in the sky
One striking, fighting miner's worth a hundred of your kind –
he's got the spirit to resist, the pride to speak his mind
Goodbye you uninspiring twat – sod off and find a spine
'cos I thought you were the furniture until I heard you WHINE!!

VIDEO NAZIS

In Rome the gladiators fought
while people slobbered in the stands
the bloodlust rose, the voyeurs wanked
with transfixed gaze and frenzied hands
then naked humans thrown to beasts
were torn apart amidst the cheers
their last entreaties drowned in blood
and wine-soaked sick sadistic jeers

And still it swells, the evil lust
centuries old and still unslaked
the cesspit of the human mind
the vampire free, unchained, unstaked
and now sick men — it's always men —
are harnessing the stinking vulture
lurking in the human soul
and flaunting it as video culture

Film makers, impotent and scared
with shrivelled pricks and sick desires
hate women so they stab their breasts
or wrench their nipples off with pliers
and hipsters in the music press
say 'What's the fuss? It's special effects!'
It's real enough in those bastards' minds —
I want to break their fucking necks!

And what of those who watch the films
of Nazis raping jewish mothers?
Do they sit there, and wank, and spout
wish they were there beside the others —
then play with children of their own
like SS butchers used to do?
Look in the mirror, nasty fan —
see Adolph Eichmann stare at you!

Now one about another sort of fascist...

ANDY IS A CORPORATIST

Andy is a corporatist
he is corpulent, often pissed
and he is friends with Flemish nazis
goes to Hitler's birthday parties
(seven times a year)
I met him at the 100 Club
he was there on business
but he couldn't start a riot
so he stayed kind of quiet
and The Business didn't play
so Andy went away
I met him in Birmingham
the day the shit really hit the fan
the fan was me and the shit was Andy
Dexys concert — really handy
broken nose is really dandy
Andy thinks it's such a laugh
to sing Horst Wessel in the bath
smash up other people's fun
make page twenty of the Sun
but I knew his time would come...
Andy's mate came up today
told me he'd been put away
'Stupid nutter, anyway'
that's all he said, then turned away
'What a waste!' that's all I'd say
'Maybe he'll change, somehow, some day'

A year of life went down the drain
then they let Andy out again
the guys inside had changed his mind
he'd left his nazi past behind
one day I met him in the pub
he'd finished with the killing club
he said he had to watch his face
'cos YOU DON'T LEAVE the Master Race . .
now Andy and his local crew
stand firm against the chosen few
he's playing in a rebel band
to spread the word across the land
and sometimes in a pissed-up haze
he talks about the bad old days
and here's his message, loud and clear—
WE'LL NEVER LET IT HAPPEN HERE!
You nazi skinheads ought to know
that you would be the first to go
'cos what THEY want is serried ranks
unsmiling clones in Chieftain tanks
no room for music, punk or skin
they'll bring the goosestep marchers in
and take our football and our bands
smash our guitars and break our hands
so no more crap about colour of skin
'cos unity's the way to win
and what our Andy says is true:
Stand firm—don't let them hoodwink you!

Working on nights at Gilbey Vintners, Harlow . . .

NIGHTSHIFT

They come from divers newtown places
boredom etched upon their faces
ready for another night on the line
And some of those walking through the door
have been there twenty years or more
their minds turned upside down through all that time

The teabreak talk is dull and tortured
tales of wives or some misfortune
minds in struggle, trying to feel
They see my emblems and retreat –
they cannot dance to the new beat
the outside world on nightshift is unreal

and in the morning when we leave
for our daily twelve hour reprieve
the nightshift warriors fear the coming night
To unloved wives and loveless lives
and newtown homes like stone beehives
the unsung heroes go in sad half light

First String Offensive

The penguins gather
on the crowded podium
who's that poseur
dinner dress and baton
You're in tune with the music
but you're not in tune with me
you look the same, you sound the same
sterile conformity
Is this the music of the ages?
Well, it was written ages ago
and they tell us that means something
and they tell us that means something

In your orchestral manoeuvres
you're not individuals –
the preening Narcissus dictates
He is your Hitler, waves his baton
and gets inflated rates
for manual acrobatics

I yearn for the interval, then bang my seat
and stamp out loud on angry feet
I came to hear some history
but this is just hypocrisy
outside there's emotion, passion and vision –
I leave you here with a sniff of derision . . . .
I thought that your music could turn my head
but the people who wrote the classics are dead.

Written by Attila aged 17
at a time of great musical
disillusionment

FACTORY GODS

(A SONG)

ageing schemers, turbanned traitors
catholic converts, mad dictators
priests in pulpits and dog collars
different kinds of ayatollahs
preaching worship, preaching violence
trust in god and keep your silence
in the pews the faithful standing
priest his pound of flesh demanding . . .

all you priests, prophets, popes and holy sages
oh you're all part of the same conspiracy
different churches, different gods may pay your wages
but you're all made in the same fear factory

see the church, tower and steeple
taste the opium of the people
jew or rasta, sikh or hindu
thousand credos to enslave you
jesus christ, superstar
born again america's latest star
the boss has bought you a company car
for services rendered to the reagan bazaar . . .

all you priests, prophets, popes and holy sages
oh you're all part of the same conspiracy
different churches, different gods may pay your wages
but you're all made in the same fear factory

for years and years you've played on our fears
controlling our hopes and our lives
your prayers cheap props and weak panaceas
and then you take your tithes
but now we look to the new holy book
of existential right —
it's written there: don't cower and kneel
take up your bed and fight
take up your bed and fight

ageing schemers, turbanned traitors
catholic converts, mad dictators
priests in pulpits and dog collars
different kinds of ayatollahs
as in ireland, divide and rule —
religion is the tyrants' tool
in the pews the faithful standing
priest his pound of flesh demanding . . .

all you priests, prophets, popes and holy sages
oh you're all part of the same conspiracy
different churches, different gods may pay your wages
but you're all made in the same fear factory
yes you're all made in the same fear factory
yes you're all made in the same fear factory

Sawdust & Empire (a song)

On the waterfront they're gathered for the feast
to pay homage to the priestess of the waves
Wider and wider the voices ring out loud
from the celebrating crowd of Albion's braves
but someone told me something that I just don't want to hear
ancestral words that fooled us for the last six hundred years
but they don't ring true any more

Sawdust and empire – the nectar of the few
so give the devil his due and break away
Sawdust and empire, with a hint of royal blue
but I won't drink with you on Empire Day

Dreams of old India, the Bible and the Host
to calm the ghost that won't be laid to rest
A distant island becomes the Holy Grail
in the spirit which revived King Arthur's quest
and you may wear her heraldry in tattoos on your arms
but it takes more than bravado now to soothe old England's qualms
'cos it don't ring true any more

Sawdust and empire – the nectar of the few
so give the devil his due and break away
Sawdust and empire, in the pub and in the pew
but I won't drink with you on Empire Day

The territories and governors have all gone now
but the bloodlust and the cliches linger on
The territories and governors have all gone now
but the bloodlust and the cliches linger on . . .

And in the theatre the fading actor stands
our destiny a nipple in his hand
And in the Stock Exchange they fly the Union Flag
though faceless bankers know no motherland
and as I love my country, the harbours and the sea
I will not serve the warmongers who seek my loyalty
'cos it don't ring true any more

Sawdust and empire – the nectar of the few
so give the devil his due and break away
Sawdust and empire, with a hint of royal blue
but I won't drink with you on Empire Day . . .

RADIO RAP

I turned on the radio this afternoon
with half a brain for a mindless tune
and if you want some mindless fun
it's always there on Radio One
The braincell level is very low
a diminished braincell ratio
and if your IQ's under five
it's just the stuff to keep you alive!
Synth pop and electrofunk
and endless hours of boring junk –
if that reflects the nation's taste
then this generation's gone to waste!
So where's the challenge? Where's the news?
Where's the ones who'll light the fuse?
Well I can see them all around
but they never make the DJ sound
'cos the senile programmers get the bird
if they hear an idea or a naughty word
so all we get to pass the days
are boring endless pop clichés
LIKE
shake your booty on the floor
hang your wombat out the door
whomp that flounder, hit that plaice
wrap that turbot round my face

RADIO RAP

save your love 'cos the girl is mine
get on down, it's disco time
OK ya and I'm alright
the happy sound on a Saturday night
And then on top of that powerful stuff
if you didn't think that was rough enough
the daytime DJs cap the lot –
THEY SHOULD BE ROUNDED UP AND SHOT!
If you want to hear a real prize prune
try Steve Wright In The Afternoon
the biggest fruit bat of them all
he'll REALLY drive you up the wall!
Like a plughole clogged with pubic hair
Young Mister Wright clogs up the air
and everyone can surely see
that he needs a lobotomy!
There's one man got the feel, it's true –
good old John Peel he talks to you –
but the most of the rest are as bland as can be
with the taste of a tench and the flair of a flea
so stuff it, stuff it, Radio One
the happy sound that's really dumb
Bring back the pirates, they had class
and STICK YOUR PROGRAMMES UP YOUR ARSE!

EROS PRODUCTS COMMERCIAL....

EROS PRODUCTS INTRODUCE THEIR EXCITING NEW RANGE INCLUDING **PENIS ENLARGERS** FOR **BLUE WHALES** GENUINE **HERNE BAY SPIKY BRAS** FULLY EQUIPPED **NATIONAL WESTMINISTER BANK TORTURE CHAMBERS** AUTHENTIC **WORLD WAR II GASMASKS** WITH THOSE **LITTLE EROTIC EXTRAS RUBBER CHEESE BOARDS LEATHER TV SETS** LIFE SIZE WET PLASTIC BLOW UP DOLLS OF **NORMAN TEBBIT** DRESSED AS A **SCHOOLGIRL** NEW **VIDEOS** TAKE YOUR PICK FROM **HUGE DONKEYS IN THE DEPARTMENT OF TRANSPORT CONFESSIONS OF A HAMSTER BREEDER MRS WHITEHOUSE'S CORRECTIVE CLASS** AND MANY OTHERS..... ALSO NEW FROM **EROS PRODUCTS** THE AMAZING **RUBBER TERRAPIN** TO REALLY TAKE YOU OUT OF YOUR **SHELL** – THIS **TERRAPIN** COMES FITTED WITH **BATTERIES** AND WITH THE **DOUGH HOOK** ALREADY ATTACHED A REAL **TREMBLER** AND SUITABLE FOR EVEN THE MOST **UNINHIBITED** OF **WOMENS INSTITUTE SOCIAL EVENINGS**.... SPECIAL INTRODUCTORY OFFER – BUY A RUBBER TERRAPIN AND GET SEVENTY THREE **SOILED** PICTURES OF **NORMAN TEBBIT** ABSOLUTELY **FREE** WITH A CHANCE TO WIN **DENIS HEALEY** OR THE **CASH EQUIVALENT** AND THAT'S A GREAT DEAL OF MONEY **I CAN TELL YOU!** ALL THIS AND MORE FROM **EROS PRODUCTS**, EPPING, **BULGARIA**. YOU DIDN'T KNOW THERE WAS AN EPPING IN **BULGARIA** DID YOU WELL THERE **ISN'T** REALLY BUT IF **YOU** HAD A **SEX DUNGEON** AND A **TACTICAL NUCLEAR WARHEAD** IN **YOUR** LIVING ROOM **YOU** WOULDN'T GIVE **YOUR** REAL ADDRESS WOULD YOU AND THAT'S ALL FROM **EROS PRODUCTS** AVAILABLE AT A **SHEEP** NEAR YOU OR PHONE **SEETHING WELLS BRADFORD 7218** AND ASK FOR **DETAILS**......

A Letter From Nigel's Mum

1, Computer Terminal Terrace
Membrum Virilae
Berks

Dear Attila,

Thought I'd drop you a line and tell you how our Nige is doing; he's a real pain these days, so cocky and arrogant you wouldn't believe. He finished his SAS training of course and then he roadied for Motorhead for a while; now he's one of Lemmy's best mates and he can drink them all under the table, no problem. He's got this Cortina with a Go Faster stripe, fluffy dice in the window, a huge cassette player with a never-ending tape of Steve Wright In The Afternoon and one of those sunstrips across the windscreen—Nige and Tracy, it says; of course, Tracy's his girlfriend—she's into Einsturzende Neubauten, origami and bondage. I know this rumour about her having leprosy but you have to be open-minded these days, don't you, and not judge by appearances; I mean, lepers are the same as everyone else, aren't they, and someone even told me they've got a natural sense of rhythm which seems a bit unlikely 'cos of all the bits dropping off but of course carpet detergents are so good these days and the maggots soon turn into flies, don't they? Anyway, Nige took up boxing, you see, and everyone could see he was really good so they sent him over to the States to fight that famous bloke who they're always making films about—Rocky I think his name is—and as if you wouldn't believe it our Nige knocked him out in the first round and now he's a real hero over there and they've got T-shirts with NASTY NIGEL on and he goes on these chat shows—once he was on the same one as Barry Manilow—and he's writing his autobiography called FROM C&A's TO LAS VEGAS. But though things are going really well I keep telling him to keep his feet on the ground and remember his roots and I've still got his SDP T-shirt and that album—what's it called?—New Gold Dream in the drawer with his teddy bear at home 'cos you never know what could happen, do you, and actually I wish he would come home 'cos I'm missing him a lot really and I know I shouldn't say this 'cos in the circumstances it sounds a bit sick what with her personal problem and all that but Tracy's really going to pieces without him, losing her head and feeling really mouldy, so if you've got the time could you write and tell him how much we're missing him 'cos I'm getting really fed up with cleaning the carpet all the time. I'll write soon with further news but till then much love from Nige's mum

Salomella

and her pet skate Trevor

THE ORACLE

A bloke who works for Pinnacle a firm that's really cynical asked me to write an article and make it really radical I know it sounds improbable and practically impossible but writing up the article I sat upon my testicle and found a little particle of testicle on my article I got a small receptacle and took it to the hospital where they looked very sceptical they said that's not a testicle it looks like a comestible you blokes are so predictable the nurse said looking cynical while waiting in the vestibule of the sceptic septic hospital a spider seized my testicle and munched it in its mandible the pain sent me hysterical it really was incredible so I clutched my aching testicle and yelled for something medical the nurse was still quite cynical as she bandaged up my testicle no need to be hysterical she said applying chemical the bandage was impractical and it exposed my oracle so the looks I got were quizzical as I left the local hospital a pig in a convertible with a mate who looked identical and really quite irascible said cover up your oracle I said it was impractical because I'd hurt my testicle and if he still was sceptical he ought to ask the hospital the particle of testicle still rested on the article which I had done for Pinnacle the firm that's really cynical the article was radical and really quite street credible and though it sounds incredible the particle was edible the one conclusion logical was that the little particle was not part of my testicle but was a small comestible as they said in the hospital by now you must be cynical this rant's become predictable and so I'll end this canticle this tale of tortured testicle mistaken for comestible I'll finish with an oracle it really is impossible to try and write an article while sitting on your testicle it makes you go HYSTERICAL!

The Duchess went pallid; the Duke stood and stared
The Colonel was livid — he spluttered and glared
and the Tory peers said 'It's a serious matter'
when the Яussians invaded the Henley Яegatta . . .

They charged in on DMs with football scarves high
Яed soccer hooligans — 'Surrender or die!'
The Dynamo Kiev boys, pissed out of their heads —
they kicked in the gates singing 'We are the Яeds!'

They danced in the fountains and pissed in the water
(which grossly offended the Archbishop's daughter)
They nicked all the strawberries and drank the champagne —
then they took off their clothes and streaked round in the rain!

They started a ruck in the private enclosure
and Alexei got nicked for indecent exposure —
took over the tannoy and put on the Clash
then they danced on the seats till they broke with a crash . . .

Then the Яedskins turned up and they started to play
and it started a party which lasted all day
and it didn't take long for the fat cats to scatter
when the Яussians invaded the Henley Яegatta!

Then they jumped in the water and nicked a few yachts
and they charged off to London at thirty-five knots
and for weeks all the hip clubs were filled with the chatter
of the day that the ЯEDS
                              took
                            the
                              Henley
                                Яegatta!

And so they're sailing down the Thames
and they hit London — WIMBLEDON

RUSSIANS ON THE Centre Court

Wimbledon Common is quiet today
and the Wombles are wombling the rubbish away
Old Madame Cholet is her usual self —
she's quietly fingering a randy young elf
but Uncle Bulgaria's started a scare:
he's just run in shouting 'Christ! Look over there!'

His trembling finger directs all their eyes
and fear soon replaces the Wombles' surprise
'cos there on the common something is amiss
a massive great malchick stands having a piss
two Soviet herberts are spraying champagne
and Vladimir is lying stoned out of his brain . . .

The RUSSIANS are here — and there's no doubt of that!
Mad Leon is waving some old toff's top hat
that lunatic Boris is dressed up in drag
and Ivan is draped in a tatty red flag . . .
They've just took the Henley, their greatest success
and what they'll do now is just anyone's guess!

70

Orinoko steps forward amidst all the fuss
and shouts 'WE ARE THE WOMBLES — you'll never take us!'
And 'We are the Wombles!' the little folk shout —
but Leon soon shows what the Яeds are about
He squashes a Womble like he was a grub
and snarls 'Show us the way to the All England Club!'

AAAARGH!

The stands are all full at the great home of tennis
and they're quite unaware of the coming Яed menace
the men's singles final is well under way
when the tannoy announces suspension of play
due to a disturbance outside at the gate
They call the police – but they've got there too late!

Vladimir and Sergei are first on the scene
climbing over the gates shouting something obscene
as the umpires tremble, all shocked and distraught
the boys from Kiev hit the great Centre Court
They sit on the turf and they swing on the net
in a scene the Controller will never forget!

THISS ISS THE LÖST TIME THAT I PLEI HJËRË EVFFÉR!!

Sergei's got a football, and with insolent glee
shouts 'Shengelia and Blokhin got nothing on me!'
so the Soviet slobs kick the football about
till they tread on the umpire and damage his gout
and the umpire moans, with a face full of woe
'Get rid of this lot – I prefer McEnroe!'

All the booze and the binge makes the Reds want to sleep
so they crash on the court in a great drunken heap
till the SPG storm in and crack a few heads
and the chief of police shouts 'Яight! Where are those Яeds?'
but the inspector says, with a very long face
'They've gone, sir, they've vanished — gone without trace!'

And that is the truth; they're nowhere to be found
it seems like they've been swallowed up by the ground
The police check the locker rooms, toilets and bars
but then come reports of a few missing cars
and the forces of order are puzzled and vexed —
where will those rampaging Яeds show themselves next?

Will it be at the Derby, the National, the cricket?
Will they sign up with Scargill as a big flying picket?
As the Tories and faint hearts stand shocked and aghast
the one thing to be sure is you ain't heard the last
So if you see a bloke with KIEV on his arm
don't try and tackle him — sound the alarm!

73

Яussians VS. THE TeHey Bittermen

Down in the Charles Bronson Arms
they strangle tigers with their scarves
and pints are held in massive palms
'cos only Southerners drink halves
They're Bradford's finest, hardest too
and in this pub you fear to tread
if you're a Cockney or a poof —
but most of all if you're a Яed . . .

Meanwhile, on the M62
the Яussian hordes are Yorkshire bound
After they wrecked the Centre Court
things got too hot to stay around
Now Wimbledon is far behind
their nicked Ford Transit's full of beer
but Leon says 'Let's stop soon, lads —
my stomach's feeling really queer!'

'OK' says Alex 'next turn-off
we'll stop and find a quiet pub
Young Leon there can have his puke
and we'll all hit the beer and grub
but listen, boys, no funny stuff —
we'll keep low profile, nice and quiet
and find a corner by the fire
I'm too hung over for a riot!'

Now we all know that History
is oft changed by the Hand of Fate
and who can know the Destiny
that lurks unseen behind the gate?
And so it was that fateful day
when Lady Luck rang the alarms
because the pub the eight Яeds chose
was that very same Charles Bronson Arms!

They trooped in quietly, one by one
and calmly stood there in a line
Vladimir says 'Яight — it's my round —
eight pints of Tetley's 'll do fine'
But just one sip of that great brew
makes Ivan splutter with a howl
'This stuff's the pits! It tastes like glue!
Pure wombat vomit! Яeally foul!'

75

A Bitterman snarls 'Hey, watch it, son —
your scruffy sort aren't wanted here
'cos we eat punks with chips in gravy
especially when they slag our beer!
And what's that tattoo on your arm?
Dynamo Kiev boys? Trotsky end?
You dirty Яussky commie shit!
Get out — and take your commie friends!'

By now the Bittermen are riled
and thirty voices shout as one
'Get out of Bradford or get killed!
Go back to Яussia, commie scum!'
'We don't want trouble . . .' Georgi says
A Bitterman growls 'Tough, Яussian git!
That Gorbachov's a filthy poof
and Dynamo Kiev are SHIT!'

Alexei grabs him by the throat —
'That's the last straw, you fascist slobs!
You don't insult our football team
— we'll make you shut your stinking gobs!
The odds they may be four to one
and you may think you're really tough
but lead on, Bittermen, lead on —
and damned be he who cries Enough!'

****

The memory lives in Yorkshire still
of how the Яeds evened the score
and as dawn broke in Bradford town
they kicked the Bittermen out the door . . .
and in the Charles Bronson Arms
they do all-night gay discos now
The Bittermen won't show their face
'cos they got splattered flat — and how!

Seething Wells spent time on the buses and as a life model before he joined the poetry scene. His poetry is as much a reaction to the "real" poets he encountered as it is an expression of his own concerns. He attacks everything 'from mainstream radio to mainstream racism' with images and inspiration drawn from a wide range of contemporary influences and delivered at manic speed.

RantS

Seething WellS

Illustrated by John Langford

London
UNWIN PAPERBACKS
Boston Sydney

RantS first published in this two book collection
in Great Britain
by Unwin Paperbacks 1985

This book is copyright under the Berne Convention.
No reproduction
without permission. All rights reserved.

UNWIN® PAPERBACKS
40 Museum Street, London WC1A 1LU, UK
Unwin Paperbacks
Park Lane, Hemel Hempstead, Herts HP2 4TE, UK

George Allen & Unwin Australia Pty Ltd
8 Napier Street, North Sydney, NSW 2060, Australia

Unwin Paperbacks with the
Port Nicholson Press
PO Box 11-838 Wellington, New Zealand

©Attila the Stockbroker and Seething Wells, 1985
Illustrations © John Langford and Porky

Cover illustration: John Langford

Designed by Graham Davis Associates
Designer Kevin Ryan
Assistant Sara Woollcombe
Typeset by Dawkins Typesetters, London

POEMS

There were three of us and ten of them
But they were poofs and we were men . . .

Capped T-shirt, capped teeth, permed hair, moustache — macho stare
You don't mess with Tetley Bittermen
We're here to stay — pal
If you can't beat us — run away
Imitation Yorkshiremen they roam the streets in packs of ten
or more
Depending on how tough they feel
which depends on how pissed they are
Adverts make converts to the Tetley Bitter cause
If told that bestiality was butch
and killing kids was cool
there'd be no brats on Northern streets
just sore and smiling puppy dogs
and packs of Tetley Bittermen
Joshua, Joshua — sweet as orange squash you are
Get it up and get them in
Only poofs drink lager
Only Southerners and women
(which is more or less the same thing anyway)
drink gin.
Real Men. Working Men.
Swill pints and pints of bitter and mild
Hard of cock and stern of jowl
they prowl the streets like rampant bulls
the poor pathetic pissed up fools
9 pints a night and fat at 40
Shredded liver and sewered mouth
But Aye! — You don't mess with our Tony!
'Cos he's *hard!* Even if he is half dead
Pisshead he may be but he's in good company
He's a Tetley Bitterman — he's *fucking hard*
Can't stop to think — he drinks his goal in life
Football on Saturday. Sex on Sunday
Work on Monday. Disco on Friday
We're here to stay — Pal
If you can't beat us — run away
Hear the Tetley Bitter call
and piss your life against a wall . . .

THIS BEING THE TRUE STORY OF THE DAY A
90FT. TALL FIRE-BREATHING REAL-MAN EATER
CAME TO BRADFORD ON A Y.O.Ps COURSE AND
GOT PASTED . . .

Screeching hate the scraper-breaking Hyper-Dragon
descends on Bradford looking for a scrap
He slaps the nut on a block of flats
'Take that!' he snorts and Bradford trembles
Doors are locked and trousers shat
Except in one pub
The Charles Bronson Arms
Where swarms of sweat-sodden Tetley Bittermen
are too pissed to hear the heavy footsteps crunching the cobblestones
like a child munching Seabrook crisps
A scaly head lisps 'Come and fight you so-called Yorkshiremen!'
The Tetley Bittermen reply as one
'Piss off git'
Oscar Wilde's got nowt on these lads
Godzilla's lost for words
'Think you're hard? You bloody dragon
Poncing in here with your Esther Rantzen haircut
and your garlic-smelling breath
Well I'll tell you this
We may be pissed
And you might be a scaly scaled up fire-breathing real-man eater
but any one of these here lads could beat you into bloody lard
with one hand tied behind us back
and us head inside a Morrisons carrier bag'
Godzilla stopped and thought (well you would do, wouldn't you?)
A Bitterman moved nearer
Godzilla runs — out the door
The Bitterman hits the floor — unconscious
Not from fear mind you but a packet of crisps
and 68 pints
All of which just goes to prove
You don't mess with Tetley Bittermen
'Cos a Tetley Bitterman never loses

DAWN OF THE ZOMBIE BITTERMEN

From the mass-graves of post-bomb North Bradford
The Bittermen climb to their feet
Then, over the bodies of non-alcoholics
they clamber up on to the street
A strange cocktail of Tetleys Ales and Strontium 235
has kept the Bittermen going strong
Awake
but not alive
It's Zombie Bittermen who walk the street
Yellowed teeth and flesh
Fall-out dust on chunky sweaters
and eyes – white – like pickled eggs
Southern poofs have died in droves
In London *nothing* moves
'Cos you're easy prey to Gamma-rays
drinking piss disguised as booze
The Zombie Bittermen march in lines
Talking in harsh nasal whines
On the poisoned air is heard the cry
'Arthur – mine's a pint'
Nothing's changed in Bradford
No, nothing's changed at all
'Cos the difference between a live and a dead Tetley Bitterman
is very, very small.

BRING BACK TONY BLACKBURN!

A SLAVERING pack of Pubescent Nubettes wets designer jeans in a tidal wave of naive sexual craving for the Mincing Fops sold like tins of beans to the Wimp-Devouring harem of Teenage sirens who scream in torrid gusts of misdirected puppy lust their Adolescent Angst for the Devil-In-Tight-Panty-Hose who oh-so-slowly licks red lips in twisted epilectic fits they strain to touch the naughty bits of the Pirrouetting Nancy Boys. These Herpes-happy Cocksure Deviationist Perverts inject infected semen into the arteries of the Common Mind. It dribbles out the ears and clogs the nostrils.

From every box of Coco-Pops a box of Rubber Noddies drops on plastic breakfast plates and the Hairy Moron caks his keks and gets SPEC-TAC-ULARLY!!!!! excited over the Pre-packaged Packages of Plastic Crap that pass as pop in the Post-punk Pre-holocaust mental vacuum situation. With fixed grins and under arm stains the point is made again and again – The Selling Point is SeX!!!!!

Must we fling this filth at our Pop Kids?

No!

I'll say not!

They must be stopped, chastised and viciously flogged on the gallows of decency, common sense and the Great British Way of Life.

OUR CHILDREN MUST BE SAVED FROM THE HERPES TIDAL WAVE.

So bring back Tony Blackburn
His sweaters and his smiles
His winning grin, his dimpled chin
His dark and sparkling eyes

So bring back Uncle Tony
And kids with lots of spots
And maybe then I'll once again
Tune in to Top of the Pops.

GIVE PEAS A CHANCE

HITLER was a vegetarian
Ghengis Khan never ate meat
Dr Crippen was a fruit juice drinker
He never knew the pleasure of eating fresh-fried liver
or of tearing off slivers of rich juicy flesh
from the gleaming bones of beasts fresh dead
It's a deep-seated human need
like breathing and SeX and the odd cup of tea
Which is why vegetarians are *twisted* little freaks
Right on! Ban the Bomb!
Get it up and get it on
Bearded and boring. Feeble and weak.
'Men against Meat' Anti-Sexist League badges on pink
    dungarees saying
'Save the Sea-slug! Legalise Flower sniffing!'
Bollock-talking thin and gawky chinless
    dribbling wimps
Droning on and on and on about 'How we're going to
    stop the Bomb
by eating nut-cutlets and chanting old Bob Dylan songs!'
Have you ever met a nice vegetarian?
No — of course you've not!
Vegetarians are worse than dogs!
and you won't find shallots in your average
    bowl of Winalot
But this idea I've got to clear up
It's KIND TO ANIMALS — OK?
and it'd save a few bob
Let's force-feed the veggies with the dog food
then feed the veggies to the dogs
Smash the System! Smash the State!
Grow your own vegetables
and vegetate.

HE/SHE'S PERFECT

HE/SHE'S perfect — can't you tell
from the fact there's a lack of bodily smell?
HIS/HER non-sexist haircut on top of HIS/HER head
Never laughs at carrion films
or jokes about the dead
HE'S ashamed of being male
SHE'S sorry she's not black
HIS/HER politics are spot on hard
not wet or lax or slack
Nothing weak. Nothing liberal
But awfully awfully right-on grey
and down-right bloody miserable.
HE went to get his consciousness raised
at a seven-day 'Men against Filth' crusade
Sits in a circle never saying 'cunt'
Never says 'prick'
Thinks that slapstick's crude and sick
That Benny Hill's a right-wing plot
That baby boys should be gassed or shot
With all the virtues HE/SHE'S got
HE/SHE'S seen as a threat to God
So watch out Lord
You're in a stew
'Cos HE/SHE'S perfect
and there isn't room for two

CADILLACS
in Bradford

Dark satanic Teddy Boys scrape reflected Brylcreem in a Cadillac's fender chrome
Home is where the heart is
Not Altamont or Memphis
These cats are Bradford's coolest
and the fattest and the oldest
Rock'n'Roll moulders in their time-warped drain-piped minds
Bill Haley never puked on stage
Cochran never swaggered like sex on crutches
No outraged parent ever said:–
'No son of *mine* will ever be a Teddy Boy!'
They forget the point of OUTRAGE
They forget that once what they said and did
shocked and horrified Vicars and Editors
Remembering the Roxy they drag drapes over heaving chests
Woodbine-wrecked they creak with pride
A Zest for death, no love of life
Seen in tunnel vision
Here in black and white and grey
and 78 r.p.m.
An Elvis Presley requiem
Rebels with receding hairlines, beerguts and failing eyesight
A thug with a mortgage – a rebel with wife and kids
Not so much without a cause as a lingering festering menopause
There are no Cadillacs in Bradford
Just old men going grey
And a brand new crop of shocking Punks
who'll end up just the same.

News at Ten used to be *really* boring
Test-tube Babies, Maggie spreading rabies, unemployment,
   Northern Ireland
But never any REAL VIOLENCE!
But now it's NEW! IMPROVED! News at Ten
Alistair Burnett goes Grecian 2000 with the NEW! ADDED!
FALKLANDS INGREDIENT!!!!!
8 out of 10 dictators recommend there's nowt like a full-scale war
for sending workers off to bed with thoughts of ENGLAND
in their cloth-capped heads
Tabloid Editors spurting lies
Benny Hill writes the Headlines
STICK IT UP YOUR JUNTA
Page 3 is on Page 5
'cos it's more fun wanking over guns and bombs
than placidly-smiling platinum blondes
It's a quick Wargasm
A war on the cheap
Save the Penguin! Save the Sheep!
Save the Falklands! Smash the Fascists!
(and their british-trained pilots
and their british-built jets
and their british-built warships)
Sold to them by the same fat-gutted Tory shits who
   screech and bleat
CRUSADE AGAINST THE FASCISTS!
Well I'm into crusades now and then
so let's start with the bastards who pollute No. 10
But No!
It's wheel out the Spitfires — Revive Vera Lynn
It's the Spirit of the Blitz
Till they bring back rationing
and conscript a garrison of 4 million women and men
Till the next time they decide it's time again
For fresh blood
on News at Ten.

8 out of 10 dictators recommend there's nowt like a full-scale war
for sending workers off to bed with thoughts of ENGLAND

The Fleet Street Shit Sheet neat little label-maker enables Joe and Mabel Smith to spot *what-goes* in the shadowy subterranean world of Subculture Cult Heroes and the Mindless Sheep who kiss the feet of the cocaine-consuming Tinsel Neroes.

AGGRO BRITAINS! apathetic youth. A spineless, pathetic, foppish group:– Gays and Communists, Anti-war feminists, long-haired punk-rocking drug-taking Anarchists, Papists and pissed-up young pagans. Half-brick lobbing, Commie-plotting Social misfits and Misfit socialists.

Inter-racial couples couple in public parks. The Sharks and the Jets get propositioned by lisping, effete randy dandies and trashed by KILLER SKINHEADS! who swarm in every inner-city brick-strewn street, amphetamine roller skates strapped to over-size feet the scourge of a nation that's gone to the dogs on its knees.

Dr Bob Martin's cure for the flea-ridden Bulldog is the short-sharp-shock of two minutes in the dock and two years of sweating in a pox-ridden prison for all who exalt the revolting, craven, disgusting and unshaven FOLK DEVILS! who corrupt and disturb the minds of the young.

The Sun's so-called journalists, quack sociologists and fascist hacks. AGGRO BRITAIN! in thirteen paragraphs. Broken noses get easy laughs from their Tit-greedy Bum-hungry highly intellectual audience of mindless Thatcher-voting zombies.

The Fleet Street Shit Sheet excretes cheap lies and The Sun cries
AGGRO BRITAIN (exclamation mark).
The only Aggro done
Is done by The Sun
To the minds of the kind of scummy prat
Who believe the crap
That the Fleet Street Shit feed them.

AGGRO BRITAIN!

HAR HAR HAR

The greaseball spivboy slob who got me the ten minute slot of so-called
POETRY READING in a 3rd rate rot-ridden half-empty hand-pumped weak beer
bordello sidles up and dribbles in my ear:—
"I thought you said you weren't political — you shit!
Oh dear — I'm afraid we can't use you again
The views you express go against the wormy beer-vomit-bigot-soaked grain
of this fine establishment
You might hurt the feelings of someone we need
Local Tory dignitaries or a member of the
National Association of Right Wing Dog-Molesting Child-Killing
Wife-Bashing Fascist Rich Pig Thug Club
and we couldn't have that now could we?
HAR HAR HAR! Really liked some of the poems tho'
Speshly when you said 'Tit'
HAR HAR HAR! 'Bum' was another one
Laughed till I came with excitement I did
But drop all that politics
All that boring commie shit
A decent pint and a bag of crisps is all that decent folk in a decent pub
want to smell or taste so shut your face and tell us some FUNNY ones
Some HO HO Bernard Fat-Gut mannerisms sonny
mention SeX and and I'll wee myself silly pissed-up and grinning clientele
Jokes about the Jews always get a laugh or two
Auschwitz is always a real bloody screamer
Party hats with razor-sharp streamers top rosy-cheeked cackling idiot-grin
Vacuum Heads
The clotted gin-and-coke set
The National Socialist Office Workers Party night-out
want
ENTERTAINMENT!!!!

from their bought and paid-for
Pet Poodle Prostitute Poet (me)
He makes them larf
HAR HAR HAR

an instant cure for mindless scum
is to drown the gibbering mindless scum
in deep-run baths of their own warm blood
that's my idea of fun.

Dawn of the Proletarian
FLESH-EATERS

THANK HEAVENS for the middle classes who in a world of revolutionary blood-bath and barbarous acts of terrorism have managed to maintain in the face of this WHIRLWIND of change a few of the things that make one say 'I'M *PROUD* TO BE BRITISH!'

Yet nowadays even this class, symbol to the world of all that marks the Anglo-Saxon as SUPERIOR TO THE FOREIGNER, is under attack. As unemployment claims area after area of the decaying inner-city, bands of WORKING-CLASS ROGUES start to maraud the outer suburbs kidnapping the sons and daughters of the Bourgeoisie as an extra source of FRESH RED MEAT.

The overstretched police force do their best but fail to respond with either the zest or the numbers necessary to curb this outburst of blood-lust amongst the masses and so it falls upon THE MIDDLE CLASSES THEMSELVES to organise vigilante groups to stop the unwashed cannibalistic hordes in their tracks, soundly smack their noses and send the scum scurrying back to their vermin-infested slums with their tails between their legs.

Barbed wire on the patio
Machine guns on the status-quo
Each of us carries a cosh and lash
And the knowledge that the Middle Class
Having survived the Blitz
Will come through smiling once again
Tho' armed with clubs and hand-grenades
We'll still find time for those things
That make life in Britain still worth living
Like washing the car, walking the dog
And even playing the odd round of golf
But EVER READY in the eyes of GOD
With a pick-axe handle and a rifle cocked
With water cannon, knives and mace
To keep the bastards in their place
For if God be an ENGLISHMAN
Then WE'RE his chosen disciples
He's alive and well in Surbiton
And he carries a loaded rifle

Imagine there's no

LENNON

In New York City a harmless hippy is blown away
By a muscle-bound dwarf with Sgt Pepper on his stereo
And Helter Skelter on his mind
The James Dean of the Man at C&A set
Meets his Lord and Maker at the hands of a lover
Whose idea of adulation was Clint Eastwood ventilation

****

The hero of the 1960's, Che Guevara with granny glasses
Drapes barricades with flaccid flowers
Drowns out the tanks advance of screaming metal
With showers of petals and the power of a record sale

****

Born the new Sid Vicious, Man
Ignore malicious historians
Lennon died for your sins only
Feeling guilty? Buy an L.P.
3 Hail Marys and give peace a chance
Dance to the watered-down Mersey Beat
His face was cute his hair was neat
A cynical sexless soft-soaped beast
Wipe your tears on John Lennon wankerchieves
Believe in divinity, he walked on water
Never drugged himself or advocated slaughter
Happiness, Man, is a warm cash register
The harder they come the richer the windfall
A transparent Jesus you could see right through
The Frank Sinatra of the Bob Dylan bank clerks
Berserked to death by a pop-eyed American
Olive-oiled hair and a Wimpey where his brain should be
Canned laughter at his coming, canned tears at his death
A crocodile executive smiles whilst he's saying cheese
And re-releases the pre-release of the humourless hymns of the King of Peace
Wipe your tears and bite your tongue
As the Mao Tse Tung of the Wolfy Smith wadicals
Is laid to rest by Beatle wig fanaticals

SHORT SHARP SHOCK

Hidey-Hi!
Hidey-Ho!
It's on your backs or on your toes
It's double time on the spot at Butlins with the Short Sharp Shock
90 days of playing soldiers, sewing mailbags, breaking boulders
Stay off the streets or we'll scrape you off
and dump you in the Butlins with the Short Sharp Shock
Cold hard sweat. Good clean fun.
Cleanliness, sobriety in the dustbin of society
Black boots, Grey shirt, Black tie, Grey socks
Welcome to Butlins with the Short Sharp Shock
The screw tightens. Rioting is frightening
So look on the bright side — ignore the truth
"Good Evening Britain — here's the news."
Mr. Burnett seems rather perplexed that people of good British stock
Have been taking what they need from shops and not paying!
It's naughty! It's wicked! It's downright un-British!
It's evil! Disgusting! It just isn't cricket
So stop it you bastards. I get so upset
Now here's an old war-film to see you to bed
The sound of parade grounds
Welcome to the clamp-down and Wonderful Radio I
Where His Master's Voice is the only song
All day and all night long
Churning out the stomp of Jailhouse Rock
Cold showers and the prison crop
We're not political
Just doing our job
We're not racist
Just doing our job
We're not robots
Just doing our job
We're the Blackcoats at Butlins
We're the Short Sharp Shock

GAME FOR A BLOOD BATH

There's something rather *English* about hitting little kiddies
as if beating children black and blue
With rulers, canes and plimsolls too
Was somehow in our blood
Can any pleasure you can name
Surpass that to be gained
From smashing in an infant's brains?
To feel their buttocks rise and swell
As you lash eight shades of hell
From squirming brat
It's the kind of pleasure that you, well
Don't often find
This side of hell

YES! Channel 4 proudly presents
'Game for a Blood Bath' folks!
The game that gives violence a bad name
And of course Violence is the name of the game
The game being:
 That barrelful of rabid monkeys
 That craaaazy blood-covered cabaret of hysterical laffs!
 That bucket of red stuff!
THE AMAZING!!!!!!!!!

GAME FOR A BLOODBATH!!!!!!!!!!!!!!!!!!!!!!!!!

Where children aged 3 thro' 10 and-a-half
Are smashed to bits by sexually-frustrated school teachers
(just for a laff!)

 So switch on the box
 Dig the aggression
 Relieve all that nervous tension
 Slowly unzip
 Smile and relax
 things happen after a violent wank.

TOLKIEN
'BOUT MY GENERATION

The gnomes all come from broken homes
Their eyes are narrow slits
To cross them means some broken bones
Or a head-butt in the naughty bits.

The pixies are an evil breed
They kidnap pet chihuahuas
Then hang them by their plastic leads
And torture them for hours.

The leprechauns like casual sex
And pulling kittens to pieces
Collecting love-bites on the necks
And spreading foul diseases

Beware Beware The Little Folk
Heed my warning well
If some dark night
By pale moonlight
You spy elf, troll or sprite
Don't linger in that leafy dell
Stomp the fucker
Then run like hell.

19¾ 4 ½

THE STENCH of cordite overlay the deeper stench of rotting fascist.
The bodies of the New Britain Militia lay twisted and askew. Arms and legs
akimbo, twisted unnatural positions as if posing in the midst of frenzied
non-aryan break-dancing. The crowds of lazy bloated flies only stirred as a
corpse was disturbed, grabbed by the ankles and hauled over to the blazing
petrol fires at the side of the road. When a corpse lay untouched the thick
blanket of insects was invisible against the matt-black of the regulation
tunic.

Overhead police helicopters swerved and chattered. Young bucks
dressed to mutilate in their black leather glad-rags screamed obscenities
at the sweating sanitation workers not caring that their monosyllabic
grunting was drowned by the blades. A black was spotted running, making
off from the water pump. The choppers banked in pursuit. Curfew control
was tiresome work when a man had a belly full of rockets and a brand new
·50 waist gun to boot, itching to be used.

The sun began to poke tamely through the yellow banks of mustard
gas and smog. The fire in the lesbian quarter still raged, shaming the orb's
feeble efforts with its fury. Soon the ovens of the Population Control camps
would add their deadly belch to the lightening sky and through asbestos
masks would be breathed the ashes of the disabled, deformed and
doomed.

As dawn finally broke the workers swarmed like mindless ants from
their corrugated hovels. The semi-darkness was broken with the flashes of
the overseers' electro-prods. Rats as big as puppies scurried for cover
under the heaps of rubbish and napalm-dried excrement and Terry Wogan's
Morning Show blasted out from a thousand loud-speakers replacing the
All-clear sirens' scalded baby-screams.

Noddy yawned and stretched. He had something to do today. What
could it be? thought Noddy, staring at the knotted hankie which he had
pulled from the pocket of his bright yellow pyjamas. 'I know,' he thought,
'I'll go ask Big Ears! He might be a grumpy old so-and-so but he's awfully
good at remembering things.' It was then that Noddy realised that he
couldn't visit Big Ears. Mr. Plod had taken him away for being naughty.
Something to do with him having 'Non-Aryan features'. Noddy laughed.
Silly old Big Ears! Always getting into trouble! Never mind, he'd clean his
teeth and then think about it.

There was a loud knock at the door. KNOCK
                                      KNOCK
                                      KNOCK . . . Just like that!
'I wonder who that could be so early in the morning?' thought Noddy.

198 4 ¾

The stench of cordite overlays
The deeper stench of open graves
The corpses of The Chosen Few
In deaths embrace with Reds and Jews
Violence marks the stiff remains
With blood, sweat and tear-gas stains
Bloated black and swollen flies
Move sluglike over staring eyes
Dragged ankle-wise to makeshift pyres
To be consumed by petrol fires

Angry choppers swerve and chatter
As coppers dressed in natty gladrags
Search for blacks and curfew breakers
With whom they'll play and mutilate
Being cop and court
And undertaker

Through banks of mustard-gas and smog
Go scurrying rats as big as dogs
Like a scalded child the All-clear screams
As workers from their hovels stream
Kept in line with dope and God
Football Pools and electro-prods
Bonfires made of Marx and Freud
And Death Camps for the Unemployed

In his bedroom as day dawns
Noddy stretches
Noddy yawns
And then from out pyjama pocket
He pulls his hankie and sees it's knotted
Noddy frowns ('cos he's forgotten)
'Oh well,' says Noddy, 'Never fear!
I'll go and ask my friend, Big Ears!'
But then as Noddy cleans his teeth
Noddy chuckles 'Silly me!'
He can't go see Big Ears today
Mr. Plod took him away

On suspicion (or so they say)
Of Red subversion and being gay
Then, above the outside roar
Come three loud knocks at Noddy's door
KNOCK
KNOCK
KNOCK
JUST LIKE THAT!
'Oh dear!' thinks Noddy, slightly yawning
'Who could that be
At this time in the morning?'

The Name of the Beast

Drivel worshippers. Berk beserkers.
Who lurk behind each dark locked door
A plague of boiling steaming sores
A mob of frogs and rabid dogs
Dense banks of yellow choking fog
A quagmire of disease and sin
Sick Cherubim and Seraphim
Shall with avenging sword
Spread the last word of the Lord
That word being BASTARDS!
RETRIBUTION! DEATH, REVENGE!
Agony without lapse or end
The sentinels of the Gates of Hell
Shall roam this planet's smoking shell
The foam-mouthed Beast shall be unleashed
The High Priestess of Babylon
And the multi-armed Devil Spawn
Of Kismet and the Dark Select
The Stallions of Gomorrah
And the microbes of Old Sodomy
On Horrid Go-Gog's Knee shall sit
The latent psychopaths
Shall fork the souls of sinners
Into pits of steaming shit
And decomposing TV dinners
We'll crucify the lying spawn of Marxist-chanting Multi-Horned
Abortionists and feminists shall curse the day they're born
The Goat shall reign
In death and pain
The sick shall die
The limp go lame
The squinting blind
The poor shall find
That rioting will pass the time

The Lion screws the Lamb that screams
The Pol-Pot Noodle junkie-feasts
Adolf Hitler shakes his cage
The new dictator storms the stage
The Devil Dog on earth shall reign
Margaret Thatcher is her name
The sick shall die
The limp go lame
The mildly-depressed insane
This is the news — the burning truth
Jesus loves the Sabre Tooth
So heed the message from above
The message being
You're gonna get stuffed.

STRIPPER

He comes on home from the hum-drum tits 'n' bum Page 3 Sun Bird plastered on locker-room doors. He's earned his hour's fun at the pub so he shovels overcooked food down his throat. "Are you off out love?"

'Yes I'm off out and no, I don't know when I'll be back: when the pubs shut mebbe.'

He gives her a stillborn kiss devoid of sex. Sex is bedtime athletics after the pubs are shut. Passion rationed twice a week. And week's the word and as cold and as effortlessly sweatlessly BORING as the beer he drinks down the pub. There's a pub in Ripper city where strippers flounce for ten pounds a night. He goes with his mates for a leer and a pint 'tho he'd never look twice at his wife the way he stares at the bored and smiling digestive biscuit packer who Pan's Peoples to an Andy Peebles pick-of-the-week. He goes home and copulates with his wife. But in his head the stripper squirms. Because sex isn't sex if it smells or it sweats or goes to the bog or shaves its legs. He copulates with his wife but in his head the stripper squirms. He's in love with supermarket charms paid for in pints of cold grey sperm.

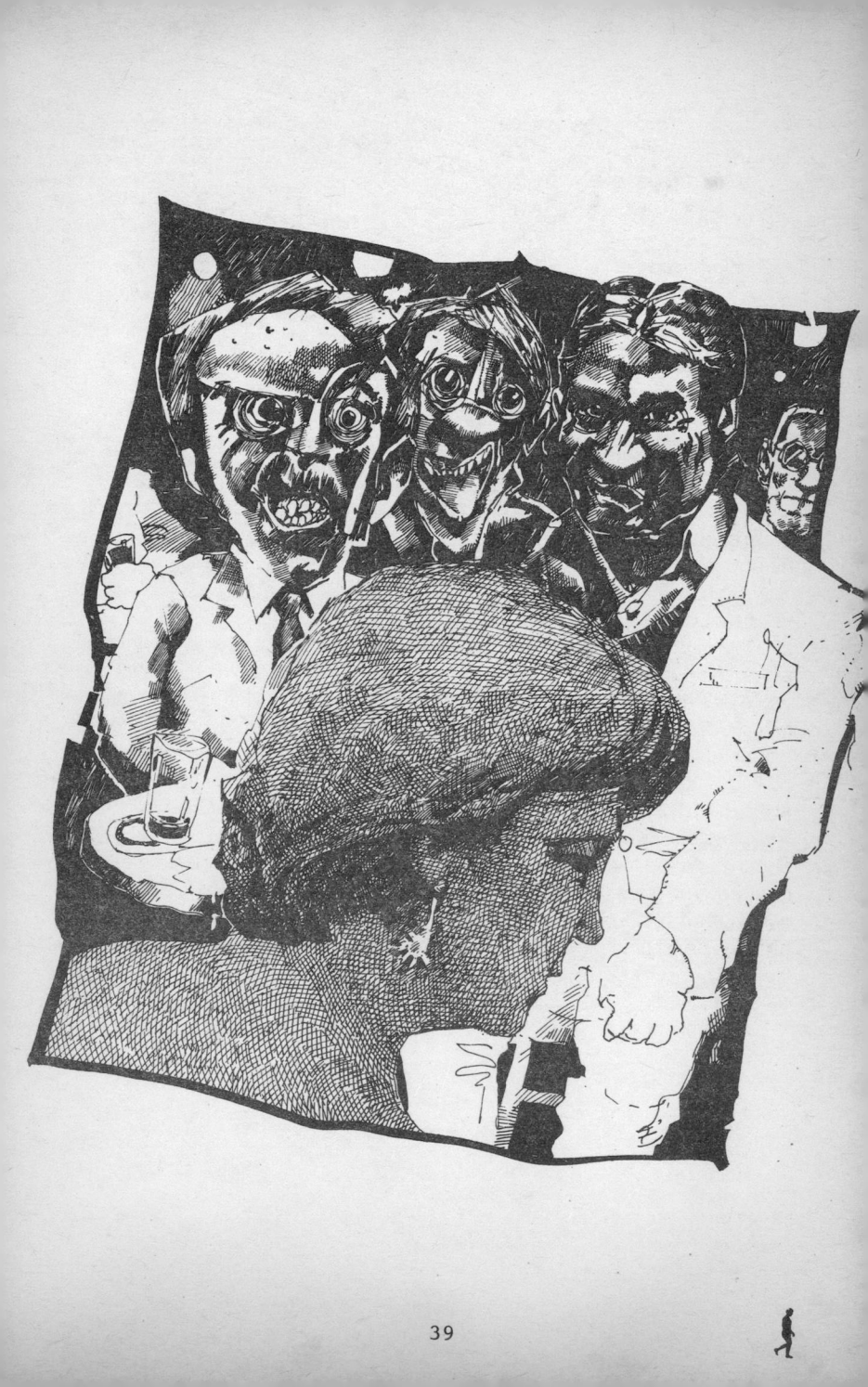

POLICE DOG

Drizzling rain, heavy fog
Being swamped by the Drug Squad
A police dog sniffs-out vitamin pills
Speed kills
These build your muscles
'What're these Punk? D'you take drugs?'
The constable snarls
The dog looks puzzled
I'm quite fond of puppy dogs
It's pigs that should be muzzled.

RODGER

Rodger Mcarthy Mcarthy Mcdoodle
Ninth-generation pedigree poodle
Crufts Supreme Champion once
Runner-up twice
13 shields and 14 cups
Is vet's-clinic-check-upped twice a week
Sleek coat
Shiny nose
'Cos Mummy knows best
And Mummy knows
That whilst Rodger glows with canine health
Money won from Doggy Shows
Grows
Wealth accumulates
Rodger's worth his weight in gold
but

Rodger got RABID

Rodger went MAD

Sad to relate that man's-best-mate
Turns nasty when the virus strikes
Come here Rodger!
Mummy said
Rodger bit off Mummy's head.

BLOOD SPURTS

Huntin' Shootin' Fishin'
Stickin' the knife in
Watchin' the blood drip
It's better than drugs old boy
A gore-spattered, 12-bore-battered
Mashed and mangled psycho trip
Grippin' a rabbit's neck between the teeth
Squeezin' 'till the eyes go Pop!
He *loves* to kill our furry friends
But . . . what about the dole-queue lot?
The scroungin' whinin' commie mobs?
'Much more fun pottin' reds
Than pumpin' rabbits full of lead
The queers and scroungers don't answer back
When freshly-stuffed on wooden plaques
Wouldn't give it a second thought
Class warfare —
Britain's National Sport.'

A Ministry of Defence spokesman today suggested how
the strangely—high incidence of fatalities by
suicide amongst the unemployed might, after all,
have its brighter side.

I'd DIE fo' me country
says a patriotic dickhead
Well go ahead
ya make me sick
Slash your wrists and slash the statistics
'The number unemployed fell today
200,000 bled away
Then they were stripped cold naked
Shaved their heads
Stopped the thrashing of severed nerve endings
by boiling the buggers in sterilised lead
Stacked them by bunkers in dumb grey ranks
Introducing— THE HUMAN SANDBAG
A major donation to the nation's salvation
The sandbag that rots
and absorbs radiation'

This depression won't fade away
It'll trickle in streams
down blood—clotted drains
One way
or another

SANDBAGS

POETRY

THE POETRY LIMPRICKS limp on endlessly
churning out poetry to be stuck up in galleries
and worshipped by the cognoscenti
Yes, Yes, Darlings! But is it ART?
Sad old men discuss their problems
like the last time they maintained erections
back in 1967
when Poetry stank of Peace & Love
The perfumed pen in the velvet glove
The Me-Generation's blubbering hit-men
Zen and the art of being boring
When adulation meant rows and rows
of slowly dozing folk in the know
The Guardian-crippled self-appointed Art Critics
Oh God – he's finished!
Yes that was *marvellous!*
AMAZING syntax!
A POWERFUL image!
Never mind it's mindless garbage
It's Poetry Darling – Art!
ME ME ME
I did this
ME and Rodger went and got pissed
back in '67
when Poetry meant the after-effects
of too much booze down well-scrubbed necks
Conversations with marijuana plants
subsidised by Art Council grants
paying for the public wank
and sold to the giggling perfumed ranks
of Laura Ashley acid-heads
Poetry choked on its own foul offal
Poetry, Man, is fucking awful
Poetry is dead
Official.